WEIRD WEATHER AND CHANGING CLIMATES

WELBECK

THIS IS A WELBECK CHILDREN'S BOOK

Published in 2021 by Welbeck Children's Books
An imprint of Welbeck Children's Limited, part of
Welbeck Publishing Group
20 Mortimer Street, London W1T 3JW

ISBN: 978-1-78312-645-3

Printed in Dongguan, China

10 9 8 7 6 5 4 3 2 1

FSC
MIX
Paper
FSC® C144853

Executive Editor: Bryony Davies
Design Manager: Emily Clarke
Designer: Darren Jordan
Picture Researcher: Paul Langan
Production: Gary Hayes

The publishers would like to thank the following sources
for their kind permission to reproduce the pictures in this
book. Key: T=top, B=bottom, L=left, R=right, C=center,
BKG=background

ARGO/University of California: 14

Climate Central: 17

Getty Images: Mark Ralston/AFP 42; /Stacey
Wescott/Chicago Tribune/TNS 33 (bottom)
Istockphoto: 5 (bottom)

Shutterstock (in order of appearance): Andrey
Armyagov 4 (top), Irin-k (4 (centre), 4 Chokchai
Poomichaiya (bottom), 4-5 Intrepix (background), 5
Simon Annable (top), 5 Aapsky (centre), 6-7 Andrey
Armyagov, 7 Intrepix 11 Wildside (top), 11 2M media
(bottom), 12-13 Irin-k, 16 Chumash Maxim (centre),
16 Sixpixx (bottom), 19 Vlada Zhi, 20 & 20-21
FloridaStock, 21 ImageBROKER, 23 ASA Studio (top
left), 23 Creatsy (bottom), 23 AfriamPOE (top right),
23 Evgeny Karandaev (bottom right), 22-23 Vchal, 24-
25 Chokchai Poomichaiya, 26-27 Ryan DeBeradinis, 27
AP (top), 27 Cammie Czuchnicki (bottom), 28, 28-29
Goga Shutter, 29 T Photography, 30 Corrado Baratta,
30-31 Phoutthavong Souvannachak, 31 Vladimir
Wrangel, 32 Robert Cicchetti, 32-33 Daniel Maurer/
EPA, 34 Ty Lim, 34-35 Marina Onokhina, 35 Ond,
Chuhastock, Anatolir, Panda Vector, 36-37 Simmon
Annable, 38 Valery Shanin, 38-39 Mathias Sunke, 39
Jim Barber, 40 Zvonimir Atletic (top), 40 Travelview
(bottom), 40-41 Harish Tyagi/EPA, 41 ArtLovePhoto,
42 TicaC (top), 43 Johann van Trodder, 43-44 Paula
French, 45 David Evison, 46 Gyvafoto, 46-47 Oticki,
47 Phant (top left), 47 Tomas Regina (centre left),
47 Gillian Pullinger (top right), Ruksutakarn Studio
(centre right), 48-49 Aapsky, 50-51 Fotos593, 51
Rich Carey (top), 51 Dmytro Zinkevych (bottom), 52
Smereka, 52-53 Vchal, 53 David Dennis (top), 53 Adam
Goodwillie Photos (bottom), 54 Praszkiewicz, 54-55
NadyGinzburg, 55 StreetVJ (top), 57 Photofusion (top),
57 Anticiclo (centre), 57 Jason Mintzer (bottom),
58 ppart (centre), 58 Pekka Nikonen (bottom), 60
Begun1983 (left) 60 (right) Daniele Cossu,

Peter Liddiard: 8-9, 10, 18, 26, 33 (top), 42, 56, 59, 61

NASA Climate 365 Project: 15

Every effort has been made to acknowledge correctly
and contact the source and/or copyright holder of each
picture, and Welbeck Children's Limited apologizes
for any unintentional errors or omissions that will be
corrected in future editions of this book.

WEIRD WEATHER AND CHANGING CLIMATES

Written by Hannah Wilson

WELBECK

CONTENTS

CLIMATE CRISIS

Our planet is warming up too much and too quickly, bringing wild weather and extreme temperatures. This is upsetting the delicate balance that supports life on Earth. This is called climate change, and it's our fault. But because we are the cause, we can be the solution, too.

STUDYING THE SIGNS

Before we take action, let's dive deep into the oceans to find out why they are heating up and how their changing temperature damages Earth. Let's shelter from superstorms, sweat it out in scorching deserts, and look up to the skies to check out the troublesome gases that are causing so many problems.

Ice caps at the poles are melting fast, sea levels are rapidly rising, and heat waves are scorching the land. The hurricanes that sweep across oceans are supercharging, and catastrophic rains are washing away farmland and towns.

Earth has warmed by about 2°F (1°C) since 1750 or so, when industrialization began and factories started to burn fossil fuels. This small increase in average surface temperature is having a big effect on the health of our planet.

FOSSIL FUELS

The coal that we burn in power plants to make electricity, the gasoline (oil) we burn inside cars, and the natural gas that heats our homes are all types of fossil fuels. Coal, oil, and natural gas formed deep underground from the fossils of plants and creatures that died millions of years ago. Fossil fuels contain carbon, and when the fuel is burned, the carbon is released as the gas carbon dioxide (CO_2).

LAYER OF GREENHOUSE GASES

A carbon footprint measures the amount of CO_2 and other greenhouse gases that an object or activity releases. For example, a fork's carbon footprint includes the CO_2 produced by mining the metal, molding it into shape in a factory, and trucking it to stores.

EARTH'S ATMOSPHERE

SUN

THE GREENHOUSE EFFECT

Our homes, cars, and factories pump out about 40 billion metric tons of CO_2 every year. This gas then wraps around our planet and lets the Sun's heat in, but not out, just like a greenhouse. Methane (see pages 52–53) is another greenhouse gas, but its greenhouse effect is a staggering 25 times more powerful than CO_2. It is released when waste in landfills rots and when cows burp grassy gas! These greenhouse gases stay in the atmosphere, so every year the "blanket" gets thicker and Earth gets hotter.

SOME OF THE SUN'S HEAT ESCAPES BACK INTO SPACE

SOME OF THE SUN'S HEAT BOUNCES OFF THE GASES AND BACK TO EARTH'S SURFACE

✖ TIP ✖

Think about the fossil fuels burned to light and heat your home and to power your car. Think about the CO_2 released by the factories that make your clothes, toys, and food. But don't panic! You can lower your carbon footprint—and this book is packed with tips to help you.

EARTH

WEATHER AND WATER

Climate change is a global problem. Weather doesn't pay any attention to the borders of different countries. Planet Earth is one huge, connected system—and the lifeblood of that system is water.

THE WATER CYCLE

Water can be a liquid, a gas (vapor), or a solid (ice), depending on its temperature. As water is warmed by the Sun, it rises as vapor, and then it cools into a liquid and falls to the ground. This happens in a constant cycle.

RAIN AND SNOW FALL FROM CLOUDS

WATER VAPOR CONDENSES TO FORM CLOUDS

SNOW MELTS AND RUNS INTO RIVERS

WATER RUNS OFF HIGH GROUND INTO RIVERS

WATER IS WARMED BY THE SUN AND EVAPORATES FROM THE OCEAN

RIVERS CARRY WATER BACK TO THE OCEAN

WATER EVAPORATES FROM SOIL AND PLANTS

WATER EVAPORATES FROM RIVERS AND LAKES

WATER SEEPS THROUGH SOIL AND ROCKS AND EVENTUALLY EMPTIES INTO THE OCEAN

WHAT IS CLIMATE?

Climate is a regular pattern of weather over a long period of time. Different places have different climates—some are hot and dry; others are cold and wet. A freak snowstorm or a heat wave every now and then does not mean that anything drastic is happening long term. But when weather gets weirder and weirder over a period of time, it's a sure sign that the climate is changing. And that means Earth could be in danger. In the following chapters, we'll find out why climate change is a problem and what can be done to fight it.

We need water for drinking and growing crops, but not so much of it that our homes flood. We need sunlight and heat for farming, but not so much that the land is scorched. When the climate changes, the delicate balance of life on Earth is at risk.

FACT
The number of droughts, floods, and other weird weather events that happen each year around the world has doubled since 1980.

OCEAN

Almost three-fourths of our beautiful blue-green planet is covered by ocean. This huge swirling mass of water powers climates and weather systems. But the world's waters are changing. Earth is warming up, and 90 percent of the extra heat is absorbed by our oceans. Today, the effects of this are dramatic. Tomorrow, they could be catastrophic.

Most of the Sun's heat
is stored in the ocean—
often for hundreds of years.
The ocean slowly releases some
of the heat by warming the air,
evaporating surface water, and
melting ice at the poles. But it
stores more than it releases,
so the ocean is constantly
getting warmer.

THE RISING SEA

Over billions of years, sea levels naturally rise and fall as continents collide and ice ages come and go. But now sea levels are rising rapidly in a short length of time. Why? It's because of expanding water and melting ice, both of which are accelerated by human-made global heating.

EXPANDING WATER

When water heats up, it expands (gets bigger). When oceans warm, this expansion raises the water level along our coastlines, causing flooding. Scientists use satellites to measure sea levels and calculate ocean temperatures. They also monitor the warming oceans by placing thermometers in them at different depths all over the globe.

MELTING ICE

The Arctic is made up of frozen seawater, so when its ice melts, sea levels don't rise, because no extra water enters the ocean. This is also true of the giant floating ice shelves that hug the coastline of Antarctica. However, as ice shelves collapse into the ocean, they no longer hold back the glaciers that flow across the land. These giant rivers of ice slowly melt into the sea, adding huge quantities of water to the ocean and raising sea levels. Mountain glaciers all over the world are also melting (compare the pictures below), pouring extra water into rivers, which then empty into the ocean, raising levels higher.

When snow and ice melt, we lose areas of white surface cover that reflect the Sun's heat back into space. On Mount Everest in the Himalayas, as glaciers retreat, they expose the frozen bodies of mountaineers who died long ago.

COASTAL FLOODING

The ocean rising by a few feet or so doesn't sound too bad, right? But if you live in a low-lying country, it's very bad news! Even a rise of a few inches would flood coastal regions all over the world. As most large cities sit by the ocean, this is a big problem for millions of people.

ISLANDS AT RISK

The Maldives, a group of islands in the Indian Ocean, is the lowest-lying country in the world—only 6 ft. (1.8 m) above sea level. Most of its 1,190 islands will be completely underwater by 2100 if sea levels continue rising at their current rate. Before that happens, though, freshwater supplies underground will be contaminated by salty floodwater washing over the land and seeping into the rock. Maldivians are fighting climate change by creating electricity from wind turbines and solar panels, instead of relying on fossil fuels.

TIDAL TROUBLE

Tides are the daily rise and fall of sea levels, caused by the Sun and Moon's gravity. Trouble begins when a high tide occurs at the same time as a storm surge—a rising swell of water up to 25 ft. (8 m) high caused by hurricanes. Water is pushed inland, flooding coastal regions. As sea levels rise, floods occur more frequently and devastate larger areas.

FACT
Flooding at high tide is up to 900 percent more frequent in the United States today than it was 50 years ago.

A rise in sea levels is flooding the state of Florida more and more frequently, swamping beachside houses. Pumps try to clear excess water, and some roads and buildings are being moved or raised. But by 2100, one out of every eight homes could be underwater.

CHANGING CURRENTS

Ocean currents are rivers of cold or warm water that continually swirl around our planet, bringing different climates and weather patterns. But the currents are slowing.

GLOBAL CONVEYOR BELT

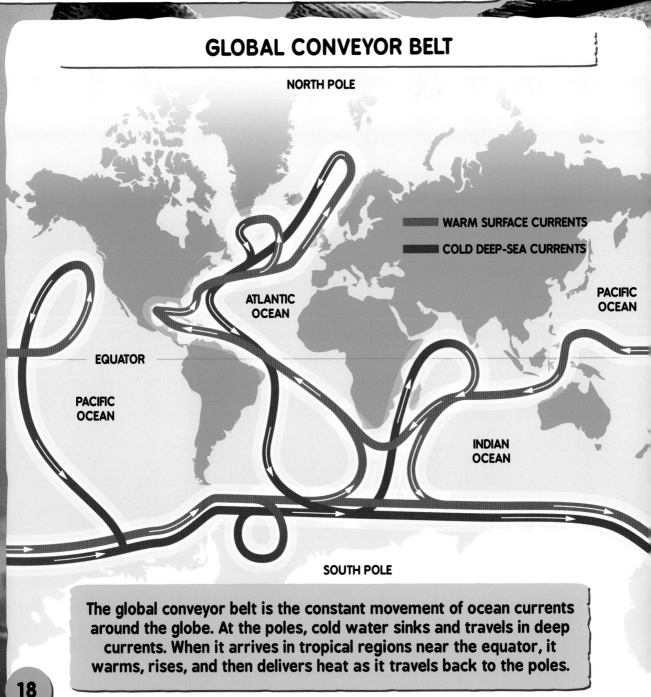

NORTH POLE

WARM SURFACE CURRENTS

COLD DEEP-SEA CURRENTS

ATLANTIC OCEAN

PACIFIC OCEAN

EQUATOR

PACIFIC OCEAN

INDIAN OCEAN

SOUTH POLE

The global conveyor belt is the constant movement of ocean currents around the globe. At the poles, cold water sinks and travels in deep currents. When it arrives in tropical regions near the equator, it warms, rises, and then delivers heat as it travels back to the poles.

ENGINE TROUBLES

The cold, deep waters at the poles are the engines that power Earth's ocean currents. As ice caps melt, more fresh water enters the polar seas. Fresh water is less dense than salty seawater, so it does not sink as easily to kick-start the deep cold ocean currents. With weaker engines, the whole system of currents is slowing.

FACT
Scientists say that the circulation of ocean currents has slowed down by 15 percent since about 1950.

Slowing Atlantic currents bring colder winters and hotter summers to Europe. The buildup of warmer water on the east coast of the U.S. may deliver superstorms and destroy populations of fish such as cod.

SLOW BUT NOT STEADY

Why does it matter that ocean currents are slowing down? The ocean stores a huge amount of the Sun's heat and distributes it around the globe, ensuring that nowhere gets too hot or too cold. Without these currents spreading heat, Earth's temperatures would be more extreme, and more areas would be uninhabitable. Warm currents also bring essential rain because warm water evaporates to form clouds.

TOTALLY **TRUE** - OR - FOOLISHLY **FALSE?**

A. It can take 1,000 years for water to travel around the globe, completing one loop of the ocean current network.

B. Cold water rises and warm water sinks.

Find the answers at the back of the book

SUFFERING SEA LIFE

As the climate changes, icy habitats shrink, seas become too warm, and oceans acidify. When fish populations suffer, so do the people who rely on fishing for food or to earn a living.

HARMFUL HEAT

Warming seas cause some fish to have too many male or too many female babies. This affects breeding and could wipe out entire populations. Plankton—tiny floating plants and animals—often prefer cooler water. If they die out, whole food chains could collapse, because the plankton are food for fish and shrimp, which are then eaten by sharks, seals, and dolphins. Polar bears are also threatened by global warming, because as the Arctic sea ice shrinks, they have less space for hunting, resting, and breeding.

ACID IN THE OCEAN

The sea absorbs some of the CO_2 from the air—about 30 percent of human-produced CO_2 ends up in the ocean. This helps reduce the greenhouse effect, but it's not all good news. As the CO_2 dissolves in seawater, carbonic acid forms. Fish and squid struggle to extract oxygen from more acidic water, and lobsters, crabs, and oysters cannot grow strong shells. As oceans acidify, corals find it hard to grow the skeletons that form reefs in tropical areas.

FACT
Coral reefs, which protect coastlines from waves, storms, and floods, are home to almost one-fourth of all ocean life.

Tiny algae live on corals, giving them energy and often color. Unusually warm seas are killing the algae, which starves the corals and turns them white. This "coral bleaching" has killed half of Australia's Great Barrier Reef since 2016.

FIGHT CLIMATE CHANGE!

✖ TIP ✖

Avoid polyester or nylon clothes—each time they're washed, up to 700,000 tiny microfibers of plastic go down the drain and can end up in rivers and seas.

The battle to protect our planet is all about reducing CO_2 by burning fewer fossil fuels. You can lower your carbon footprint with a few simple steps.

WHAT YOU CAN DO

✓ Reduce, reuse, and recycle your stuff. This means fewer fossil fuels are burned to power the factories that make clothes, toys, food packaging, and all kinds of other things.

✓ Switch off. Save energy to save the planet.

✓ Take your own water bottle and shopping bag.

✓ Reduce the amount of new things you buy.

✓ Check out thrift stores for second-hand treasures.

✓ Reuse as much as possible, and then donate your stuff so others can reuse it.

✓ Recycle—don't dump in polluting landfills.

REDUCE

REUSE

RECYCLE

AWESOME ACTIVITIES

Save money—and the planet—by making your own gifts, wrapping paper, and cards. Then get busy with some simple ocean experiments.

GREETING CARDS

Stick pictures from old magazines onto scraps of thick paper.

BEACH CLEANUP

Collect some litter from the beach to stop it from trashing the ocean.

ACID OCEAN

Find two similar seashells. Put one in a glass of water and one in a glass of white vinegar (which is acidic). Compare them after 24 hours.

ICEBERG MELT

Fill a glass with water and ice cubes (icebergs). Mark the glass to show the level of the water. Does it rise when the ice has melted?

ARE YOU SEA SMART?

Find the answers at the back of the book

Test your knowledge . . .

1. What increases when sea levels rise?

 A. Number of fish

B. Coastal flooding

C. Tropical storms

2. What happens to ocean currents as Earth gets warmer?

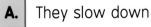 **A.** They slow down

B. They speed up

C. They disappear

3. What is formed when CO_2 dissolves in the ocean?

 A. Arctic acid

 B. Atlantic acid

 C. Carbonic acid

WILD WEATHER

Global warming can be hard to understand. While some parts of the world are getting hotter and drier, others are frozen by icy storms or drenched by heavy rains. That's why we talk about a changing climate. As Earth heats up, our weather is getting wet, windy, weird, and often wild.

Since the 1950s, Earth has experienced heavier rainfall and more frequent storms. Sewers and drains overflow, unable to cope with sudden, intense downpours. Rivers struggle to hold the extra water, bursting their banks to flood the surrounding land.

WILD WINDS

When hot, moist air rises from tropical oceans, it can gather into swirling storm systems. These hurricanes, also known as cyclones or typhoons, deliver devastating rain, wind, and waves.

HUGE HURRICANES

Many large rain clouds swirled together over warm oceans gather more energy from winds powered by Earth's rotation. These hurricanes, perhaps 300 mi. (500 km) wide, storm across the ocean, gaining even more energy from the water.

COOL AIR DESCENDS

RINGS OF THICK, SWIRLING CLOUDS

WARM AIR SPIRALS UP AROUND THE EYE

EYE—A CALM CENTRAL AREA 20–40 MI. (30–65 KM) WIDE

FACT
In 2017, Hurricane Maria doubled in strength to a deadly Category 5 hurricane in less than 24 hours. The island of Dominica in the Caribbean Sea was devastated.

When Cyclone Nargis struck Myanmar in Southeast Asia in 2008, it sent a surge of floodwater 25 mi. (40 km) inland. More than 84,000 people died and 53,000 went missing. Some towns and villages were wiped out.

TWISTING TORNADOES

A tornado is a rotating funnel of air that spins to the ground from a storm cloud. Every year from March to June, these storms rampage through "Tornado Alley" in the United States. Warming seas in the Gulf of Mexico are creating more and more storm clouds. Scientists are unsure if this will bring more tornadoes—it depends how winds are affected. But the warming could shift Tornado Alley eastward, toward more densely populated regions.

FACT
At least 1,200 tornadoes hit the U.S. each year. Spinning at up to 300 mph (480 kph), they tear through homes, whisk away cars, and can even suck water from rivers!

EXTREME RAINFALL

As the ocean warms, more and more moisture rises from its surface. Our skies store the water, whisk it along in the wind, and then dump it on towns and fields—sometimes with devastating consequences.

DESTRUCTIVE DOWNPOUR

In cities, rain can't sink into roads and buildings, so it washes into drains, which often overflow with harmful waste water. In the countryside, heavy rains destroy farmers' crops, causing food shortages. Water-soaked hillsides can slip, sending landslides several miles wide crashing downhill. Deforestation increases landslides because the soil is no longer knitted together with tree roots.

FACT

Rainfall in the Amazon rain forest has increased over the past few decades as a direct result of the warming of the Atlantic Ocean.

SUDDEN SOAKING

Most rain is made from water that has evaporated from the ocean. But evaporation also happens on land, as moisture rises from soil, plants, rivers, and lakes. As Earth warms, this can happen very quickly, leaving areas sucked dry of all moisture. Weirdly, in parts of India, some droughts that have left the land parched end with intense rain. The land has been baked so hard that it cannot easily absorb the water, so it floods. Climate change will bring more of these unpredictable weather events.

A monsoon is a season of heavy rain that happens in many tropical countries. Increasing amounts of moisture from the warming Indian Ocean are fueling monsoons in India. Water is needed for growing food, but too much can wipe out crops.

TOTALLY TRUE - OR - FOOLISHLY FALSE?

A. Experts are 90 percent certain that climate change will bring heavier and more frequent rainfall.

B. A monsoon season is a period of severe drought.

Find the answers at the back of the book

RIVER FLOODING

Rivers tumble down hills and rush down mountains, then meander over lower and lower ground until they empty into the sea. As rains increase and the hills are soaked like sponges, rivers flow more furiously, causing more flooding.

BURSTING BANKS

With heavier rainfall running off high ground and rising sea levels pushing up from the coast, rivers are struggling to contain the extra water. Clearing vegetation for building or farming doesn't help, because soil—no longer held together by roots—washes into rivers, leaving even less space for the water. When the rivers finally burst their banks, muddy floodwaters devastate nearby towns, cities, and fields.

FACT
Flash floods happen very quickly, sending walls of water up to 20 ft. (6 m) high rushing across the land.

LIVES AT RISK

Poorer countries around the equator will suffer the most from climate change. These tropical regions will face higher temperatures, more powerful hurricanes, heavier rain, and flooding. When rivers burst their banks and swamp homes and farmland, people in poorer countries do not have the money to start new lives elsewhere. They struggle to find food and rebuild homes, and the lack of clean water causes diseases such as cholera.

Four hundred million people in 11 countries along the Nile River in Africa depend on the river. As rainfall increases in the Ethiopian Highlands (the river's main source), many homes and farms are being devastated by more extreme flooding.

DEEP FREEZE

So if our planet is warming, why are some parts of the world being buried in snowstorms or frozen by icy blizzards? Climate change causes more extreme weather—and that can mean extreme cold, too.

FACT
As weather gets weirder, hailstones will get bigger. Prepare for balls of ice the size of oranges!

POLAR VORTEX

The icy winds that swirl around the poles are known as polar vortices. In January 2019, the Arctic polar vortex swept much farther south than usual, freezing parts of eastern North America and dumping snow in the normally warmer southern United States. The vortex was affected partly by a change in winds caused by warming seas, but mostly by a disruption in the jet stream.

JET STREAM JITTERS

The jet stream is a fast-flowing "river" of wind that occurs where cold polar air meets warmer tropical air. As the poles warm because of global warming, the temperature difference at this boundary decreases, causing the jet stream to slow or move in sharp bends. One of these bends pulled the Arctic vortex southward, bringing the deep freeze to North America in 2019. As jet streams slow, vortices and other weather systems will hang around longer than usual.

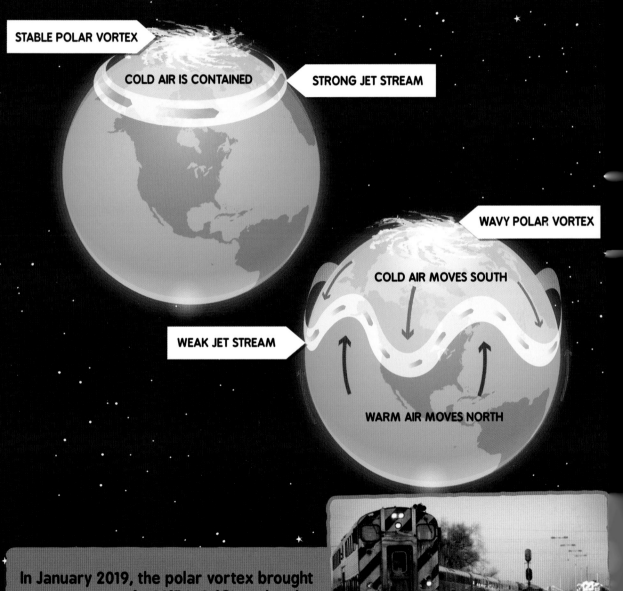

STABLE POLAR VORTEX

COLD AIR IS CONTAINED

STRONG JET STREAM

WAVY POLAR VORTEX

COLD AIR MOVES SOUTH

WEAK JET STREAM

WARM AIR MOVES NORTH

In January 2019, the polar vortex brought temperatures of −23°F (−31°C) to the city of Chicago. Train tracks had to be set on fire to stop them from freezing!

FIGHT CLIMATE CHANGE!

Think green to stop weather from becoming extreme! Here are suggestions for how you can make a difference and take care of planet Earth.

WHAT YOU CAN DO

Think about how things are made. Plastic uses oil, drilled from below the ground and processed in factories. Use less plastic to produce less CO_2.

✓ Cut back on single-use plastic (plastic that is used once before being thrown away or recycled).

✓ Travel by bus, train, or bike—instead of by car—to reduce your carbon footprint.

✓ Organize a school bake sale to raise money for places affected by flooding or hurricanes.

✓ Choose unpackaged produce at the grocery store.

✓ Take charge of your classroom's recycling.

✓ Use your own lunch box for takeout or leftover food.

FACT
It can take 1,000 years for some types of plastic to break down in a landfill!

AWESOME ACTIVITIES

Turn your eyes to the skies to watch for wild weather.
Then make some storms of your own!

! Ask an adult to help you with any cutting.

RAIN CATCHER

Collect rain in
the bottom half
of a plastic bottle.
Every day, dip in
a ruler to measure
and record any
rainfall, then
empty the bottle.

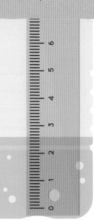

STORM IN A GLASS

Squirt shaving
foam onto water
in a glass.

HOMEMADE HURRICANE

Pour some water into a
bowl, stir it quickly around
and around, and add
drops of
food
coloring.
What
happens to
the coloring?

Add spoonfuls
of water with
food coloring
onto your foam
"cloud." How
much water
can it hold
before it
"rains"?

ARE YOU A WEATHER WHIZ KID?

Test your knowledge . . .　　　　　　Find the answers at the back of the book

1. Where is Tornado
Alley?

A. Mexico

B. Myanmar

C. United States

2. What increases the
risk of river flooding
and landslides?

A. Deforestation

B. Planting trees

C. Cholera

3. What does the weather
become because of
climate change?

A. More extreme

B. More predictable

C. Calmer

HEAT

The 2°F (1°C) rise in global temperature since the start of industrialization (see page 8) has caused oceans to swell and the weather to become wet and wild. But the extra heat does something else, too—it makes things hot! In some places, daytime temperatures are soaring, and droughts, heat waves and wildfires are making some parts of Earth uninhabitable for plants, animals, and humans.

As Earth heats up, droughts become more extreme, and farmers struggle to find water for crops and cattle. This causes food shortages and, in the worst cases, famine—a widespread lack of food that can cause the death of thousands of people.

DROUGHT

Overall, climate change brings an increase in rainfall. But in some parts of the world, it brings less rain. These places are drying up, and people are struggling to find enough water to drink and to grow crops or raise animals.

DRIER AND DRIER

Droughts are a normal part of dry seasons in many parts of the world. But climate change is making some droughts more extreme. As ocean and air currents change and slow down, there is less rainfall in some areas and dry seasons hang around for longer. Warmer temperatures mean that more moisture evaporates from the land, drying out vegetation and soil. The sudden, heavy downpours caused by climate change run off the surface of the hard, baked land. This runoff may fill rivers and lakes, but it doesn't soak into the soil where it is needed for thirsty crops.

FACT

The Sahara is the world's biggest warm-weather desert. It has expanded by 10 percent since 1920, partly because of climate change.

TROUBLING TREE RINGS

Scientists can study tree rings to identify when droughts occurred in the past. Thick rings indicate a period with plenty of water for growth; thin rings indicate dry periods. Using this method, NASA scientists have figured out that a drought in the eastern Mediterranean from 1998 to 2012 was the worst one in the past 900 years. Human-caused climate change was partly —or possibly largely—to blame.

The year 2017 was the driest year in South Africa since records began in 1933. The dams that supply water to Cape Town almost completely dried up, causing severe water shortages. The Western Cape province introduced emergency water rationing.

HEAT WAVES

If temperatures continue to rise at their current rate, some parts of Earth will be too hot for humans to live in by the end of this century. Extreme heat waves harm humans, destroy crops, and spread disease.

TOO HOT TO HANDLE

Humans keep cool by sweating —releasing moisture from our skin into the air. But we cannot sweat easily if the air is already very humid (full of moisture). So when a heat wave strikes humid regions, people get dangerously hot. About 1.5 billion people live in the south Asian countries of Pakistan, India, and Bangladesh—many in poverty. It's been predicted that by 2100, the heat and humidity in some parts of this region will be so high that if people go outside unprotected, they will die within a few hours.

Many people around the world have to work outside for long periods in fields or on construction sites. They will be extremely vulnerable to the effects of heat waves.

DEADLY DISEASE

Tropical diseases begin in the tropics—the hot region around the equator. But as human activity warms Earth, the tropics are spreading farther north and farther south of the equator—and so are the diseases. Malaria is carried by a tropical mosquito. As the insect's habitat expands, the disease will spread to more areas of the world.

FACT

When an extreme heat wave hit India in 2015, about 2,500 people died. The capital, New Delhi, neared 113°F (45°C), causing some roads to melt.

TOTALLY **TRUE** - OR - FOOLISHLY **FALSE?**

A. Green energy uses renewable resources that don't run out, such as wind, sunlight, and ocean waves.

B. Green energy uses energy produced in power plants from coal, oil, or natural gas.

Find the answers at the back of the book

WILDFIRES

Wildfires are nature's way of clearing vegetation for new growth, but climate change is bringing more than nature can handle. And when fires break out, they spread faster and farther, fueled by drier conditions.

CHANGING WEATHER PATTERNS

In the Pacific Ocean, water on the surface is warmed by the Sun and then pushed west by wind. How strong or weak these winds are makes a big difference to the water temperature—and to the resulting weather.

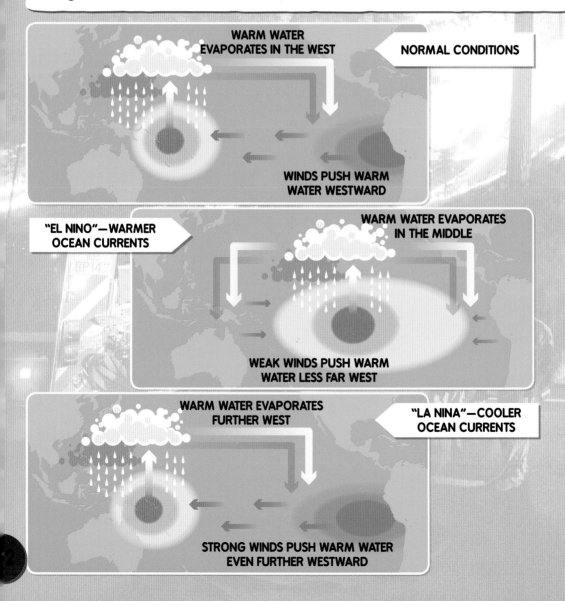

WARM WATER EVAPORATES IN THE WEST

NORMAL CONDITIONS

WINDS PUSH WARM WATER WESTWARD

"EL NINO"—WARMER OCEAN CURRENTS

WARM WATER EVAPORATES IN THE MIDDLE

WEAK WINDS PUSH WARM WATER LESS FAR WEST

WARM WATER EVAPORATES FURTHER WEST

"LA NINA"—COOLER OCEAN CURRENTS

STRONG WINDS PUSH WARM WATER EVEN FURTHER WESTWARD

CALIFORNIA BURNING

In 2018, a series of 8,527 wildfires ravaged the western state of California for several months. More than 80 people died, and almost 14,000 homes were destroyed. Wildfires in California have been getting worse. In 2020, they burned more land than any previous year on record. It costs millions to put out the fires and rebuild. Wildfires also release carbon dioxide (CO_2), increasing the greenhouse effect that leads to further climate change. The smoke contains toxic gases that harm humans and pollute our environment.

FACT
California's 2018 wildfires released 68 million metric tons of CO_2—almost the same amount generated from electricity production in the state in a year.

Weaker winds and warmer currents in the Pacific are a phenomenon called "El Nino." Stronger winds and cooler currents are called "La Nina." These occur naturally, but climate change is intensifying them. In 2018, a supercharged La Nina made California hotter and drier, which had a direct impact on deadly wildfires.

WILDLIFE AT RISK

Creatures all over the world are affected by climate change as their habitats shrink or move. It's not just polar bears in the Arctic that suffer as our planet warms. Animals in hot climates are struggling with empty water holes, scorched plants, and dangerously high temperatures.

HUNGRY AND THIRSTY

As severe droughts become more common, many water holes in southern Africa are drying up. This is a huge problem for elephants, which need to drink 40–80 gal. (150–300 L) of water every day. The lack of water and excess heat affect plant life, too. In Australia, shrubs and grasses are changing or disappearing altogether. Because of this, many rock wallabies are no longer getting a healthy diet, and their population is reducing.

FACT
If Earth continues to heat up at its current rate, 80 percent of mammals and 86 percent of birds in a 925,000 sq. mi. (2.4 million km²) area of southern Africa will be at risk of extinction by the 2080s.

ON THE MOVE

Shrubs in Canada and Alaska are creeping closer to the warming Arctic, followed by the moose and snowshoe hares that eat them. On mountainsides, plants and animals are climbing higher as snowlines retreat. Mackerel in the Atlantic have swum northward to cooler waters near Iceland. Not all wildlife adapts easily, and towns often block the path of animals forced to move. As spring arrives earlier, flowers are blooming too soon for the bees that feed from and pollinate them.

Turtles bury their eggs in sand, and the temperature determines whether hatchlings are male or female. In many of their habitats, warmer sand is causing an imbalance of females.

African wild dogs rely on cool mornings and evenings for hunting. As temperatures rise, their pups go hungry. From 1989 to 2000, about five pups in each den survived for at least a year. By 2012, when it was 2°F (1.1°C) warmer, only three survived.

FIGHT CLIMATE CHANGE!

Think about the food and water you consume, and go green to battle Earth's warming. Vegetables are better for the planet than meat, and water is precious, so go easy on the faucet!

WHAT YOU CAN DO

Saving water also saves energy, because electricity is used to clean and pump your water.

✓ Turn off the faucet when brushing teeth, and take showers, not baths.

✓ Use a green-energy supplier to power your home if possible.

✓ Avoid electric fans and air-conditioners when you can. Keep cool by closing curtains and blinds.

✓ Reduce your carbon footprint by eating less meat.

✓ Collect rainwater for watering plants.

FACT

Our "water footprint" is how much water we use for washing and making all the things we consume. In the U.S., the average person's daily footprint is around 2,060 gal. (7,800 L)—about 85 bathtubs!

AWESOME ACTIVITIES
Go veggie for a day, and follow these steps to keep wildlife happy in the heat!

MEAT-FREE MEAL
Make a vegetarian pizza.

BIRD BATH
Fill a shallow tub or tray with stones and water for birds.

FACT

A vegetarian diet produces about 8.4 lb. (3.8 kg) of greenhouse gases every day. A meat-rich diet produces 15.9 lb. (7.2 kg)—partly because cows burp methane! (See page 52.)

BEE GARDEN
Plant an outdoor pot with bee-friendly flowers.

HOT OR COLD?
Put a thermometer outside in the shade. Record the temperature at the same time each day for a week during different seasons.

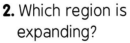

ARE YOU A HEAT HOTSHOT?
Test your knowledge . . .

Find the answers at the back of the book

1. What does runoff do?

- **A.** Soak into soil
- **B.** Flow over ground
- **C.** Form whirlpools

2. Which region is expanding?

- **A.** The Arctic
- **B.** The tropics
- **C.** Australia

3. What is happening to wildfires?

- **A.** They are becoming more frequent
- **B.** They are getting smaller
- **C.** They are spreading more slowly

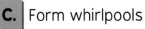

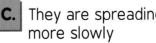

AIR

Swirling all around us and moving in and out of our lungs, air is a vital life force—for us and for our planet. But factories, power plants, and cars are pumping harmful gases into the air we breathe. Some are toxic. They damage our health and can devastate plants, animals, and wild spaces. Other gases are nontoxic to our bodies, but by wrapping around Earth, they cause devastating climate change.

Vehicles and power plants belch out the nontoxic greenhouse gas carbon dioxide (CO_2), as well as toxic carbon monoxide, sulfur dioxide, and nitrogen oxides.

TREE POWER

Trees help our environment because their roots hold soil together, preventing floods and landslides. But trees protect us in another even more important way. They pump oxygen into the air and suck up harmful carbon dioxide (CO_2).

FACT

Every year, Earth's forests suck up more than 2 billion metric tons of carbon. One-fourth of that is absorbed by the Amazon rain forest, which covers 2.3 million sq mi. (6 million km^2) and produces more than 20 percent of Earth's oxygen.

OUR ATMOSPHERE

The air that wraps around Earth is mostly nitrogen gas. About one-fifth is oxygen—the gas that plants and animals need for life. Almost 1 percent is argon, and other gases make up even tinier slices. Carbon dioxide, that troublesome greenhouse gas, is less than one-tenth of 1 percent of our air.

THE GASES OF EARTH'S ATMOSPHERE

ABOUT 78% NITROGEN

ABOUT 0.04% CARBON DIOXIDE

ALMOST 21% OXYGEN

ALMOST 1% ARGON

PLANTS THAT PROTECT

When we breathe, we absorb oxygen and expel CO_2. At night, plants and trees also take in oxygen and give off CO_2, but they reverse this process during the day. As they photosynthesize, they use sunlight to absorb CO_2 and produce oxygen. Overall, they absorb much more CO_2 than they produce, and they release 10 times more oxygen than they use. So this makes plants and trees great planet protectors.

Deforestation is bad news for our planet. When trees are chopped down, they can no longer absorb harmful CO_2. In fact, when they rot or are burned as fuel, they release it. In the Amazon rain forest, an area three times the size of Wyoming has been deforested since 1970, mainly for cattle grazing.

FACT

If an object or activity is "carbon neutral," it means that no CO_2 is released when making or doing it. To achieve this, some people "offset" their carbon footprint by planting CO_2-sucking trees.

METHANE

Like carbon dioxide (CO_2), methane is a greenhouse gas that traps heat on Earth. But landfills and farms are pumping it out at an alarming level. And there's an even greater climate calamity lurking in the frozen permafrost at our poles.

WHAT IS METHANE?

Methane is a nontoxic flammable gas, 25 times more powerful than CO_2. It is released by rotting organic matter (material from plants, bacteria, or tiny creatures) when there is no oxygen present. Methane leaks from trash buried deep in landfills and from the rotting grass inside cows' stomachs, which is released in farts or burps! The natural gas used to heat our homes is also up to 90 percent methane.

FACT

Worldwide, farm animals produce about 15 percent of all human-caused greenhouse gases.

THAWING PERMAFROST

At the poles and high in the mountains, the ground is permanently frozen. The soil of this "permafrost" contains organic matter. As icy regions warm, the permafrost is thawing. The organic material within is being released, and it rots. This process releases thousands of metric tons of methane (and CO_2) into the air, accelerating climate change.

FACT
One study predicts that by 2100, the thawing permafrost could have released 37 billion metric tons of CO_2 and 1 billion metric tons of methane.

It's easy to see the methane that bubbles up through lakes, but it's not easy to collect and measure it. Scientists visit lakes in Canada, where bubbles of methane are trapped in the ice like frozen jellyfish. After the ice is chipped away, the gas can be funneled into bottles.

CITY SMOG

Do you ever breathe in smelly, hazy air that gives you a sore throat or cough? That's air pollution. In cities, cars and factories pump out toxic gases such as carbon monoxide. Inside many homes, black smoke billows from cooking fires. Air pollution causes all kinds of illnesses.

THE PARTICULATE PROBLEM

Car exhaust pipes and factories also release tiny bits of soot called particulates. These are too small to see, but the tiniest ones are the most harmful. PM 2.5s are particulates that are smaller than 2.5 micrometers—about 30 times narrower than a hair on your head. Unlike larger particulates, PM 2.5s are not stopped by nose hairs or expelled with a cough. They can pass through the walls of the lungs and into the bloodstream, where they travel around the body and cause health problems.

B.

Dutch inventor Daan Roosegaarde's 23 ft. (7 m) tall air purifier sucks in city smog and pumps out clean air. This "smog vacuum cleaner" also collects the dirty particulates and compresses them into gemstones that are used to make jewelry. Filtered smog is about 40 percent carbon—the same stuff that diamonds are made of!

CLEAN AND GREEN

Gasoline-powered vehicles emit polluting smoke and soot because their engines burn gasoline (a fossil fuel). Electric cars and buses powered by hydrogen fuel cells do not use combustion (burning) for power. These "zero emission" vehicles do not pollute our cities, but they do use energy to create the electricity or hydrogen that powers them. To combat climate change, this energy should come from a green, clean, renewable source.

FACT
All 16,000 buses and all 22,000 taxis in Shenzhen, China, are electric. Making the taxis electric reduced carbon emissions by 440,000 metric tons a year!

TOTALLY TRUE - OR - FOOLISHLY FALSE?

A. Electric cars and buses are much noisier than gasoline-powered vehicles.

B. Certain trees, such as elms and ashes, can filter out air pollutants, reducing city smog.

Find the answers at the back of the book

ACID RAIN

Remember the cycle that transports water around the world through oceans, rivers, and the air? (See page 10.) Because it's all connected, when the air is polluted, it means that water becomes polluted, too.

TOXIC RAIN, SNOW, AND DUST

Lightning produces nitrogen oxides, and volcanoes belch sulfur dioxide, but most of these gases come from people burning fossil fuels. When they mix with oxygen and water in the sky, they form acids that fall to the ground in rain, snow, and hail.

WINDS BLOW THE ACID PARTICLES LONG DISTANCES

THE ACID FALLS WITH RAIN, SNOW, OR EVEN DUST

THE GASES MIX WITH WATER AND OXYGEN TO FORM ACIDS

POWER PLANTS AND VEHICLES EMIT NITROGEN OXIDE AND SULFUR DIOXIDE GASES

RIVERS, LAKES, AND SOIL ACIDIFY, HARMING FISH, INSECTS, PLANTS, AND TREES

HABITATS IN DANGER

Acid is corrosive—it wears materials away. Pummeled by too much acid rain, marble statues appear to melt and iron railings rust. But our wild spaces suffer the most. As soils acidify, nutrients are worn away. Plants and trees struggle to grow, and they even die. The acidic rainwater that runs off the land into lakes and rivers kills fish and their eggs. Delicate insects also die as their habitats acidify, affecting animals further up the food chain.

Graveyards of trees carpet the landscapes of areas affected by acid rain.

FACT
In the 1980s, sulfur emissions from power plants in Britain blew across the North Sea and fell in acid rain in Norway, wiping out salmon and trout populations. Today, Norway pours 45,000 tons of lime into its rivers and lakes every year to make them less acidic.

FIGHT CLIMATE CHANGE!

We can't control the wind, but we can control what we pump into it. So take a deep breath —we're going green to keep our air clean.

WHAT YOU CAN DO

Reducing energy reduces the pollution created to make it. Think about indoor air, too. What pollutes your home?

✓ Try eco-friendly liquids for cleaning, not harmful chemical sprays.

✓ Walk or bike to school to avoid pollution-heavy cars.

✓ Turn the heat down—put on another sweater instead!

✓ Use an extractor fan and open a window when cooking.

✗ Say no to woodstoves and open fires.

AWESOME ACTIVITIES
Investigate the air quality in your home, then plant some natural air purifiers. They make great presents, too!

POLLUTION PLATE
Smear petroleum jelly over a white piece of plastic. After three days, use a magnifying glass to examine any particulates stuck to it.

PLANT PURIFIER
Bring ivy, spider plants, and peace lilies inside to filter your indoor air.

TREE TIME
Plant a tree to suck up CO_2.

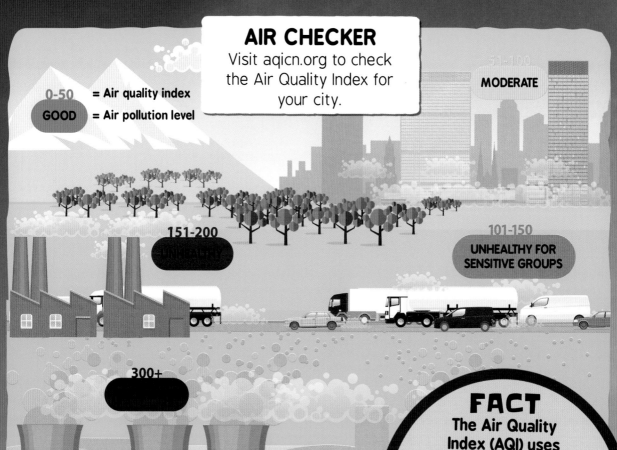

AIR CHECKER
Visit aqicn.org to check the Air Quality Index for your city.

0-50 = Air quality index

GOOD = Air pollution level

51-100
MODERATE

101-150
UNHEALTHY FOR SENSITIVE GROUPS

151-200
UNHEALTHY

201-300

300+

FACT
The Air Quality Index (AQI) uses measurements of particulates and polluting gases to give a color-coded number for cities around the world. Green means clean air, yellow means moderate, and red is unhealthy.

ARE YOU AIR AWARE?
Test your knowledge ...

Find the answers at the back of the book

1. What is the most common gas in our atmosphere?

A. Nitrogen

B. Oxygen

C. Carbon dioxide

2. What produces methane?

A. Rotting organic matter with oxygen

B. Rotting organic matter with no oxygen

C. Cow pies

3. Why are very small particulates of pollution harmful?

A. They can pass through the walls of our lungs

B. They are invisible

C. They smell bad

59

A GREEN FUTURE

Your future is in the hands of politicians and business leaders around the world. They can prevent a climate catastrophe by cutting carbon emissions. But they need to act seriously—and right now! You can help persuade them.

THE OZONE BATTLE

In the 1980s, scientists realized that certain chemicals in aerosol sprays were eroding the ozone layer. This layer of ozone gas shields us from the Sun's ultraviolet rays, which can cause skin cancer. Governments banned the chemicals, and slowly the holes in the ozone layer began to close up. Proof that if governments work together quickly, they can protect our planet!

FACT

In August 2018, Swedish 15-year-old Greta Thunberg was worried about a heat wave and forest fires in northern Europe. Day after day, she sat outside government buildings in Stockholm to protest against climate change, and she sparked a worldwide movement.

Today, Greta travels (by train or boat) to different countries, telling politicians: "I want you to panic . . . And then I want you to act."

CRAZY COOLING?

There have been many outlandish ideas for cooling Earth by reflecting heat away from it—for example, painting the roof of every building white or growing crops with shiny leaves. But this meddling could do more harm than good. Here are some more crazy ideas.

GIANT SPACE MIRRORS SO MORE HEAT IS REFLECTED INTO SPACE

CLOUD THINNING SO CIRRUS CLOUDS TRAP LESS HEAT

AEROSOL INJECTION OF REFLECTIVE PARTICLES INTO THE STRATOSPHERE SO HEAT BOUNCES OFF

MARINE CLOUD BRIGHTENING: SHIPS SPRAY SALT SO CLOUDS REFLECT MORE HEAT

OCEAN MIRROR EFFECT: SHIPS RELEASE TINY BUBBLES SO THE SEA REFLECTS MORE HEAT

The best way to stop global warming is to address the cause and reduce greenhouse gas emissions. In 2015, many countries committed to the Paris Agreement. It aims to prevent global temperatures from rising more than 3.6°F (2°C) above pre-industrialization levels this century. This will require governments to make dramatic changes right now.

GLOSSARY

ACID
A chemical substance, often found dissolved in water, that can break down other materials or react with them. Lemon juice and vinegar are acidic. Sulfuric acid is a powerful acid that can cause burns.

ATMOSPHERE
A layer of gases around a planet, moon, or star that is held in place by the force of gravity.

CARBON DIOXIDE (CO$_2$)
A colorless, odorless gas released when fossil fuels such as coal, oil, and natural gas are burned. Volcanoes produce CO$_2$, and animals and humans breathe it out.

CARBON FOOTPRINT
The amount of carbon dioxide and other greenhouse gases that an object or activity produces during its whole "lifetime."

CLIMATE
The average pattern of weather in a place over a long period of time.

CONTAMINATED
Spoiled or made dirty by the addition of a harmful or unwanted substance.

CONTINENTS
Huge sections of land that move around on top of Earth's hot liquid interior. There are seven continents, most containing a collection of different countries: Africa, Antarctica, Asia, Australia, Europe, North America, and South America.

DEFORESTATION
The cutting down of many trees, reducing the size of a natural forest.

DROUGHT
A long period of time with no or very little rainfall.

ECOSYSTEM
The plants and animals of a certain area that live together and affect each other. A small pond or a huge forest each have their own complex ecosystem.

EMISSION
A substance, often a gas, that is released into the atmosphere, often from a factory or vehicle.

EVAPORATE
To change, when heated, from a liquid to a gas.

FOSSIL FUEL
Oil, natural gas, or coal, which formed underground millions of years ago from decomposing plants and animals. Fossil fuels contain a large amount of carbon.

GILLS
Slit-like openings on a fish's body. Water passes out through the gills once oxygen has been taken from it.

GLACIER
A large mass of ice that moves slowly downhill over land, often through mountain valleys.

GREEN
Environmentally friendly and aiming to protect, not harm, planet Earth.

GREEN ENERGY
Energy created from renewable resources (such as wind, wave, and solar power) rather than from nonrenewable, polluting fossil fuels.

GREENHOUSE GAS

A gas such as carbon dioxide or methane that wraps around our planet, keeping it warm. The gases create the same effect as a greenhouse—they let heat in but not out.

HEAT WAVE

A period of unusually hot weather.

ICE AGE

A period lasting thousands of years in which varying amounts of Earth's surface are covered with ice. As there is ice at Earth's poles today, we are currently experiencing an ice age.

INDUSTRIALIZATION

When countries or large groups of people move from a rural farming life to mining and gathering materials and making products inside factories.

LANDFILL

An area or pit where nonrecyclable waste is dumped and stored.

METHANE

A powerful greenhouse gas produced when plant matter decomposes with no oxygen present. Natural gas is mostly methane.

OXYGEN

A colorless, odorless gas, mainly produced by plants. Animals and plants need oxygen to live.

PARTICULATE

A tiny bit of a material, often released into the air when the material is burned.

POLES

The North Pole, in the Arctic, is Earth's most northerly point. The South Pole, in Antarctica, is Earth's most southerly point.

POLLINATE

To transfer pollen (a powder-like substance) from a plant's male part to another plant's female part. This fertilizes plants, enabling them to create seeds to grow new plants.

REPRODUCTION

When creatures create babies, usually by the joining of a male and a female.

SEA LEVEL

The average global surface height of the ocean. Satellites can determine the average distance the surface lies above Earth's center. Tide gauges measure local sea levels in different regions around the world.

SOLAR PANEL

A panel with special materials that absorb energy from sunlight and turn it into electricity.

THAW

To melt when warmed, changing from hard frozen matter into a liquid or soft material.

TOXIC

Poisonous and likely to cause harm to plants or animals.

TROPICAL

Of or relating to the hot, wet regions surrounding the equator, which is the imaginary line circling Earth's middle.

VAPOR

Tiny drops of liquid, often water, that hang in the air. Mist is water vapor.

WIND TURBINE

A rotating device with blades that are spun by the wind to create energy that can be turned into electricity.

ANSWERS

PAGE 19
OCEAN: TOTALLY TRUE OR FOOLISHLY FALSE?

True: It can take 1,000 years for water to travel around the globe, completing one loop of the ocean current network.

The second statement is false.

PAGE 23
ARE YOU SEA SMART?
1B, 2A, 3C

PAGE 29
WILD WEATHER: TOTALLY TRUE OR FOOLISHLY FALSE?

True: Experts are 90% certain that climate change will bring heavier and more frequent rainfall.

The second statement is false.

PAGE 35
ARE YOU A WEATHER WHIZ KID?
1C, 2A, 3A

PAGE 41
HEAT: TOTALLY TRUE OR FOOLISHLY FALSE?

True: Green energy uses renewable resources that don't run out, such as wind, sunlight, and ocean waves.

The second statement is false.

PAGE 47
ARE YOU A HEAT HOTSHOT?
1B, 2B, 3A

PAGE 55
AIR: TOTALLY TRUE OR FOOLISHLY FALSE?

The first statement is false.

True: Certain trees, such as elms and ashes, can filter out air pollutants, reducing city smog.

PAGE 59
ARE YOU AIR AWARE?
1A, 2B, 3A

FIND OUT MORE

Check out **worldwildlife.org** to find out how the World Wildlife Fund is tackling climate change to protect our animals.

Ask an adult if you can look up **Greta Thunberg**'s official Facebook or Twitter account to get some green inspiration.

Become a Climate Kid with NASA at **climatekids.nasa.gov**.

Explore your world with videos, fact sheets, and more at **kids.nationalgeographic.com**, and find out how to reduce, reuse, and recycle at **berecycled.org** and **wastebuster.co.uk**.